A TRUE BOOK

W9-DHI-176

Volcanoes

ELAINE LANDAU

Children's Press®
An Imprint of Scholastic Inc.
New York   Toronto   London   Auckland   Sydney
Mexico City   New Delhi   Hong Kong
Danbury, Connecticut

Content Consultant

K. Shafer Smith, Ph.D.
Associate Professor, Center for Atmosphere Ocean Science
Courant Institute of Mathematical Sciences
New York University
New York, NY

Library of Congress Cataloging-in-Publication Data

Landau, Elaine.
  Volcanoes / by Elaine Landau.
     p. cm. -- (A true book)
  Includes index.
  ISBN-13: 978-0-531-16886-8 (lib. bdg.) 978-0-531-21354-4 (pbk.)
  ISBN-10: 0-531-16886-7 (lib. bdg.) 0-531-21354-4 (pbk.)

  1. Volcanoes--Juvenile literature. I. Title. II. Series.

  QE521.3.L386 2009
  551.21--dc22   2008014795

Produced by Weldon Owen Education Inc.

7 8 9 10 R 18 17 16 15 14   62

Find the Truth!

Everything you are about to read is true *except* for one of the sentences on this page.

Which one is **TRUE**?

T or F A volcano can affect the weather.

T or F Volcanic eruptions are always violent explosions.

Find the answers in this book.

Contents

THE BIG TRUTH!

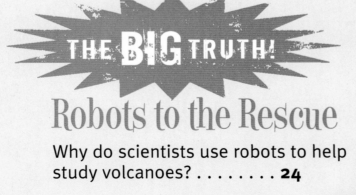

Robots to the Rescue

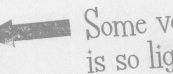

Some volcanic rock is so light it can float.

Mount Etna in Sicily, Italy, towers over the city of Catania. It is Europe's largest and most active volcano.

It's a Volcano!

Imagine you live 30 miles from an **active volcano**. One morning, you hear a tremendous blast. It is so loud that people hear it as far as 3,000 miles (4,800 kilometers) away. Huge amounts of gas, ash, and rock are blown into the air. Red-hot lava flows. A thick, dark cloud of dust and smoke blocks out the sun. It is still morning, but it looks as if night is falling.

Light from some volcanoes is so bright that a person can read at night, one mile away.

Semeru Volcano is the highest volcano in Java, Indonesia. It has been erupting almost constantly since 1967.

A seemingly peaceful volcanic mountain has come to life. Now those living nearby must quickly escape. Buildings, crops, and transportation systems are at risk as well.

Erupting volcanoes can affect life for miles around. Hot smoke and ash may clog the air, making it difficult for plants and animals to survive. Volcanic ash and gases are sometimes blasted high into Earth's upper **atmosphere**. There, air currents carry the clouds of ash great distances.

Volcanic ash can cause wildly colorful sunsets.

Clouds of volcanic ash and debris in the upper atmosphere block sunlight. Earth receives less of the sun's energy. That can lower the planet's temperature. The year 1816 was called "the year without summer" because of cooling caused by Indonesia's Tambora Volcano. This cooling lasted for a few years.

In 1991, the eruption of Mount Pinatubo cooled the temperature of our entire planet. Mount Pinatubo is in the Philippines.

Mount Eden in Auckland, New Zealand, is an ancient
inactive volcano. Past eruptions created a bowl-shaped crater
more than 160 feet (50 meters) deep on the volcano's peak.

CHAPTER 2

How Volcanoes Occur

Volcanoes are openings, or vents, in Earth's **crust** through which melted rock and gases escape. The melted rock and gases come from deep underground. They may seep out slowly, or explode out in a sudden blast. The rock then cools and hardens. Sometimes it builds up to form a mountain around the vent. We call these mountains volcanoes, too.

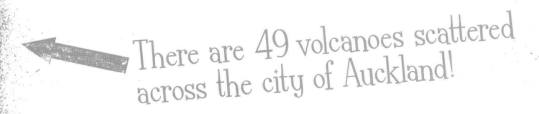

There are 49 volcanoes scattered across the city of Auckland!

What Is Inside a Volcano?

Below Earth's thin crust is a thick, hot layer of rock called the mantle. In some places the mantle melts. This melted, or molten, rock is called magma. Magma has a lower **density** than the rock surrounding it. This causes magma to rise toward Earth's surface, like a cork would float to the surface of water. On its way up, magma collects to form pools called magma chambers.

As magma rises, gases within it expand. The gases foam up like bubbles in a soda bottle that has been shaken. This can cause enough pressure to make the magma shoot out of the ground. That's an eruption! Magma that flows out of a volcano is called lava.

A major eruption releases more energy than an atomic bomb.

Inside an Erupting Volcano

During an eruption, lava and gas can escape from more than one vent.

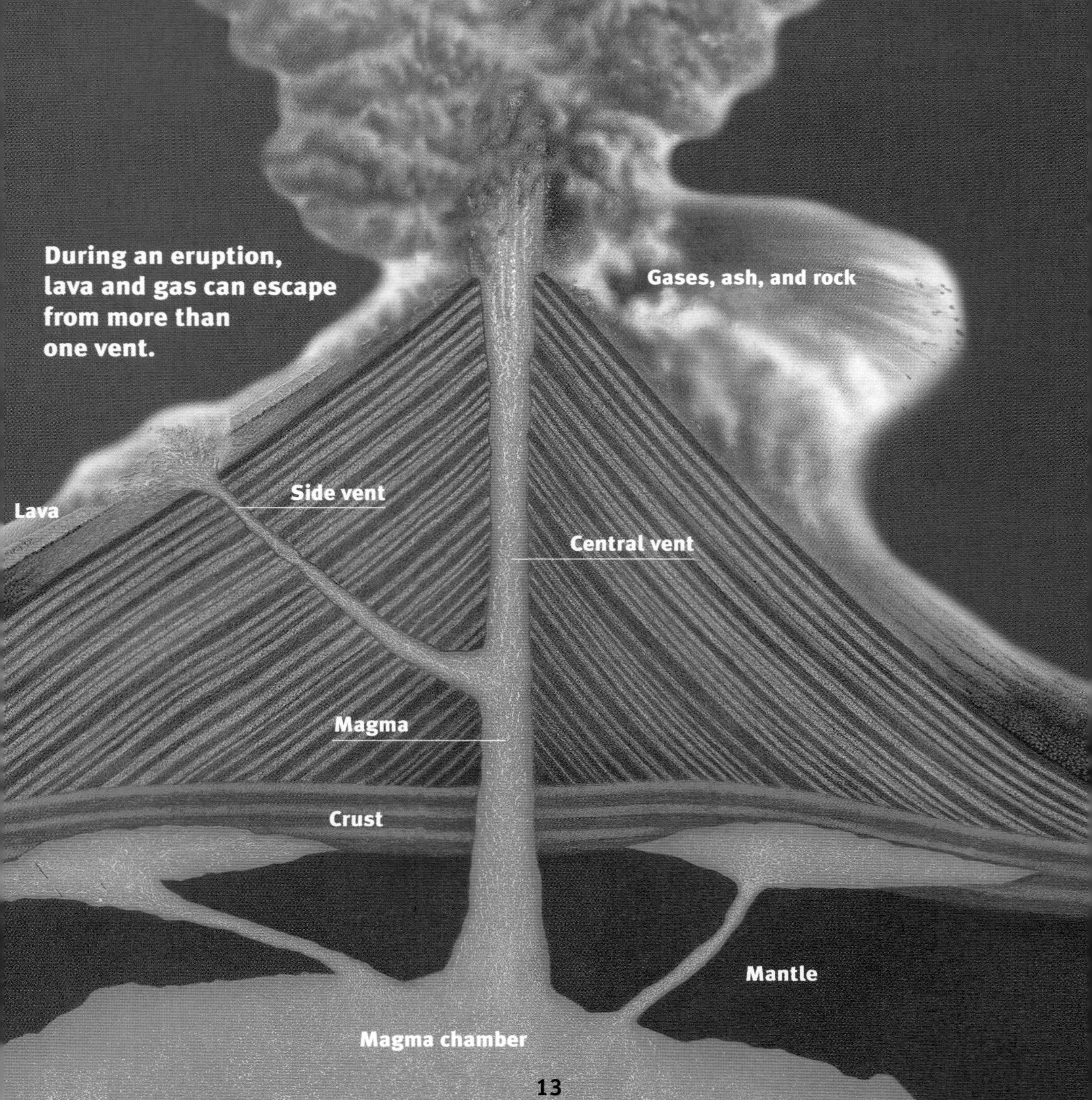

Gases, ash, and rock

Side vent

Lava

Central vent

Magma

Crust

Mantle

Magma chamber

Where to Find a Volcano

Earth's crust is broken into large slabs of rock called **tectonic plates**. The plates fit together like huge puzzle pieces. These plates do not stay still. They are like rafts, slowly moving across Earth's surface. Most volcanoes form where two of these plates meet.

Most of Earth's volcanoes are located on a series of plate boundaries in the Pacific Ocean called the Ring of Fire.

The Ring of Fire

Pacific Ocean

KEY
▲ Active volcano
Ring of Fire

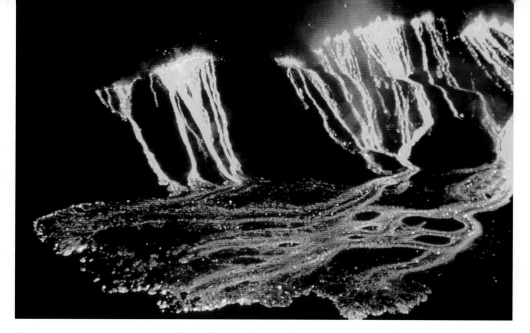

Lava can move at speeds of 60 miles (100 kilometers) per hour.

Not all volcanoes form at the edges of plates. Some form over hot spots. These are places where super-hot streams of magma flow upward through the mantle. The hot rock melts holes in Earth's solid crust. A hot spot stays still, while the plates keep moving. When a hot spot is under the ocean, this process forms a string of volcanic islands. The Hawaiian islands formed from volcanoes that erupted over a hot spot in the Pacific Ocean.

Creating Shapes

Because volcanoes erupt in different ways, they can look very different. When magma is thin, gases escape easily. Lava oozes out rather than explodes. Thin lava forms a gentle bump in the ground called a shield volcano.

When magma is thick, trapped gases build up pressure and then explode with a powerful blast. Explosive, gas-filled lava can shoot up and settle back to form a cinder-cone volcano. Tall, steep mountains formed by layers of lava, ash, and rock are called stratovolcanoes, or composite volcanoes.

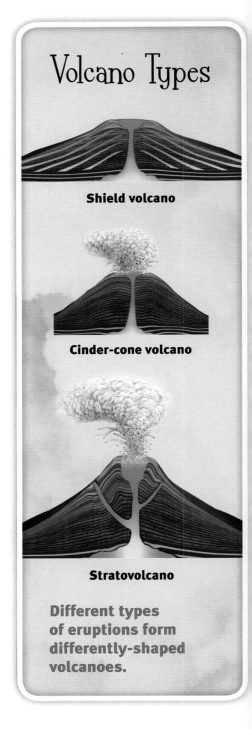

Volcano Types

Shield volcano

Cinder-cone volcano

Stratovolcano

Different types of eruptions form differently-shaped volcanoes.

Under the Sea

Many of the world's volcanoes are located on the ocean floor. In 1977, scientists found "black smokers" in ocean-floor volcanoes for the first time. These are chimney-shaped vents that spew hot water. The water is heated by underground magma. It is sooty-looking, giving the vents their name. Extraordinary life forms thrive around the black smokers. They don't need the energy of the sun. Instead, they live on minerals in the hot water!

The plume from the eruption of Mount St. Helens rose to a height of about 16 miles (26 kilometers).

CHAPTER 3

Wake-Up Call

Mount St. Helens Volcano, in Washington State, had been inactive for 123 years. Then, in March 1980, the area was shaken by a series of small earthquakes. Steam rose from the mountain. A huge bulge formed on its side. Scientists recognized the signs of an upcoming eruption. People were warned to **evacuate**. Unfortunately, not everyone listened.

The Mount St. Helens eruption was the deadliest in U.S. history.

Crumbling Mountain

At 8:32 A.M. on May 18, 1980, a large earthquake shook Mount St. Helens. The north side of the mountain collapsed. Thick magma spurted out. Clouds of ash shot into the air. An **avalanche** of rocks and mud flowed down the mountain. It was followed by a fiery stream of gases, ash, and rock. This stream reached a speed of about 80 miles (130 kilometers) per hour.

Snow and ice on the mountain melted, creating mudflows. The mud buried everything in its path.

The heat from the eruption burned trees as much as 15 miles (24 kilometers) away.

Fifty-seven people died in the eruption. About 200 homes were destroyed by mudflows. Bridges, roads, and railroad tracks were wiped away. Close to the eruption, ash rained down. It collapsed roofs under its weight. Ash clouded the air and stopped trains and airplanes from running. Cars, trucks, and buses were forced to a standstill as their air filters became clogged.

Tens of thousands of acres of forest were destroyed. Vast areas of cropland were buried under a thick layer of ash. About 7,000 larger animals such as deer, elk, and bears were killed, as well as untold numbers of smaller animals. Large numbers of birds died in the hot, ash-filled clouds. Winds carried the ash miles through the air. In cities 250 miles (400 kilometers) away, the sky grew gray.

Time Line of Famous Eruptions

79 A.D.
Mount Vesuvius

The ancient city of Pompeii, Italy, is buried under tons of volcanic ash.

Before 1883

Krakatau

1883
Krakatau

The eruption blows away two-thirds of the island of Krakatau (krah-kuh-TAOW) in Indonesia.

After the eruption, cleaning up and rebuilding started immediately. It was an enormous job. Workers had to dig up nearly one million tons of ash to uncover roads and airports. Homes, businesses, and roads had to be rebuilt. Despite many small eruptions following the May explosion, life around the volcano slowly returned to normal. Tourists stopped fearing the area and began to visit the incredible volcano.

1943
Paricutín

In Mexico, a new volcano grows out of a cornfield. It erupts for nine years. Lava covers two villages.

1991
Mount Pinatubo

The eruption of Pinatubo in the Philippines kills nearly 350 people.

Manipulator

Camera

Gripper

Robots to the Rescue

The job of a **volcanologist** can be very dangerous. Since the 1990s, scientists have worked to develop robots to help research volcanoes. *Robovolc*, a remote-controlled explorer, works inside a volcano while its human operators control it from computers at a safe distance.

Robo Gear

Robovolc's three cameras gather and send data. There is also a manipulator—a jointed arm that ends in a gripper. The gripper can pick up rock samples as large as 6 inches (15 centimeters) across.

Great Grip

Springs on Robovolc's six big wheels allow the robot to move across steep and unstable surfaces.

Deadly Gas!

The gases let off through volcanic vents may be as hot as 1,100 °F (600 °C). They can be deadly. Robovolc collects gases and measures how quickly they escape from the vents.

People harvest sulfur from Ijen Volcano in Indonesia. It is used to make products such as paints, paper, and textiles.

CHAPTER 4

A Useful Blast

Volcanoes have extraordinary power. They can cause massive destruction and many deaths. Mountains may be created by them, and whole landscapes changed forever. Yet volcanoes also provide us with rich sources of minerals and help life thrive in some surprising ways.

The steaming acid in this crater lake would eat through a person's skin in minutes.

The Canary Islands are volcanic islands off the northwest coast of Africa. Crops such as onions grow well in the rich volcanic soil.

Good Earth

During an eruption, volcanic ash can be deadly and destructive. Afterwards, it can be helpful. Ash contains many minerals that help plants grow. The ash mixes with soil to make fertile land for plants. Wind, water, and even animals can help mix the ash into the soil. After the eruption of Mount St. Helens, gophers dug their way up through the ash layer, mixing it with soil.

Volcano Homes

In Cappadocia (Kap-uh-DOHK-ee-uh), Turkey, ancient volcanoes have been worn away by wind and water to create a landscape of steep cliffs and tall cones. For hundreds of years, people have carved their homes directly into the soft volcanic rock. Today, there is even a hotel!

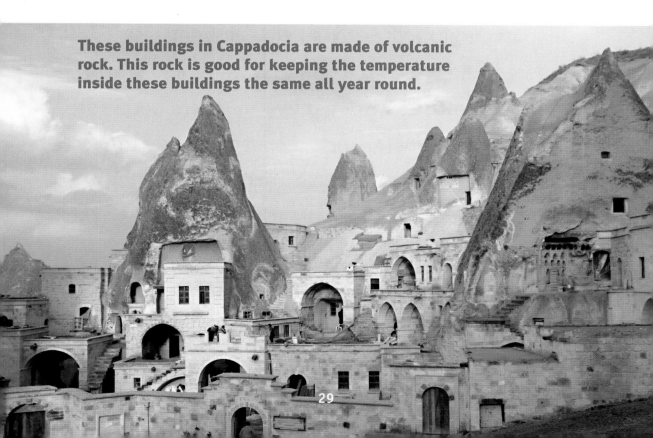

These buildings in Cappadocia are made of volcanic rock. This rock is good for keeping the temperature inside these buildings the same all year round.

Iceland has been using the energy from hot springs as a source of power for more than 60 years.

Earth's Heat at Work

Deep underground, Earth's heat can bring underground water to a boil. Hot water and steam rise to the surface, where they can create hot springs and **geysers**. They can also be used to heat homes and produce electricity.

At **geothermal** power plants, steam from under the ground is used to turn huge **turbines**. This produces electricity with very little pollution. Geothermal power produces a small but growing portion of the world's electricity.

Hot Spot

Humans are not the only ones to enjoy a hot bath. In Japan, a kind of monkey called a Japanese macaque is often found soaking in hot springs. The macaques can survive in cold, northerly climates. This has earned them the nickname "snow monkeys." Scientists have found that the young monkeys and their mothers were the most likely to take a dip. Unsurprisingly, the monkeys took baths most often during the winter.

Stromboli Volcano in Italy is known for explosive eruptions of lumps of hot rock called volcanic bombs. This type of eruption is now called a "Strombolian eruption."

CHAPTER 5

Volcano Warning!

If you lived near an active volcano, would you have time to escape an eruption? Scientists are working hard to make sure the answer is most often "yes." For many years, volcanologists have studied eruptions. They have found important warning signs that tell them when a volcano is about to blow its top.

Stromboli has been erupting almost continuously for about 2,000 years!

On the Lookout

Before an eruption, magma begins to rise inside a volcano. Rising magma can cause small earthquakes, which may signal an upcoming eruption. Scientists measure earthquakes with an instrument called a **seismograph**. Magma can also cause the sides of the volcano to bulge out. Volcanologists can measure this with instruments called **tiltmeters**.

Volcanologists test lava with special probes. They study lava samples to learn how volcanic rocks form.

Volcanologists also monitor changes in gas emissions. An increase in carbon dioxide (CO_2) and sulfur dioxide (SO_2) is a warning signal. A temperature increase of the magma also alerts scientists to possible danger.

Volcanologists have developed volcano warning systems. Based on the amount of volcanic activity they observe, they may issue an "advisory," a "watch," or a "warning." A warning means that people should get out of the area immediately!

In 2008, volcanic fumes killed six people camping on an Indonesian volcano.

CAUTION

VOLCANIC FUMES ARE HAZARDOUS TO YOUR HEALTH AND CAN BE LIFE-THREATENING
VISITORS WITH BREATHING AND HEART PROBLEMS, PREGNANT WOMEN AND YOUNG CHILDREN SHOULD AVOID THIS AREA

Saving Lives

Volcanologists monitor eruptions closely. They use satellite data to track lava and ash flows. Finding the speed and direction of flows helps them determine who needs to evacuate, and when.

Volcano prediction is not an exact science. Every volcano behaves a bit differently, and each one may act in surprising ways. Yet the more information scientists collect about a volcano, the better their chances of making accurate predictions. Accurate predictions can save thousands or millions of lives.

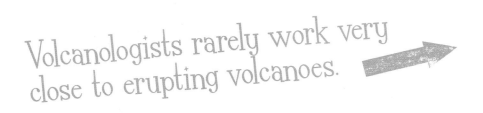

Volcanologists rarely work very close to erupting volcanoes.

Volcanologist's Gear

Helmet to protect head
against falling rocks

Visor to allow vision
while keeping out heat

Heavy gloves to protect
hands when collecting
rock samples

Fireproof suit to
protect against heat

Volcanologists
occasionally get close to
an active volcano to gather
data. Their knowledge and
protective equipment
help to keep them safe.

In New Zealand, Mount Ruapehu (roo-uh-PAY-hoo) is popular with skiers, snowboarders, and hikers. After an eruption in 1996, the ash plume lingered for weeks.

CHAPTER 6

Survival Tips

There are many people in the world who live near an active volcano. This is particularly true in countries such as Japan, Indonesia, and the Philippines. Farmers grow crops on the rich, volcanic soil near volcanoes. People enjoy camping, climbing, or skiing on the slopes of volcanoes. However, there can be real risks.

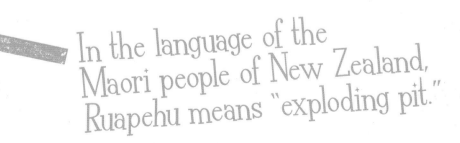

In the language of the Maori people of New Zealand, Ruapehu means "exploding pit."

Be Prepared

The first and most important survival tip is to listen to warnings and evacuate when told to do so. Governments in high-risk areas often have warning systems to let people know about eruptions. They have evacuation plans to help people leave an area quickly and safely.

In 1984, the Mayon Volcano in the Philippines erupted. About 73,000 people had to be evacuated.

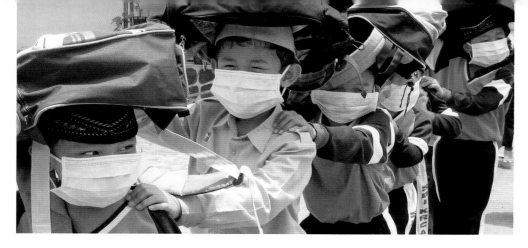

In areas near active volcanoes, people carry out regular evacuation drills. These Indonesian children are learning how to act in an emergency.

Communities have taken other steps to lessen risks. Roofs are built to be strong enough to support a load of ash. Protective walls are built to direct the flow of lava away from towns.

Families in danger zones should have a disaster kit. This should include bottled water, first-aid supplies, a radio that runs on batteries, a flashlight, and canned food. Dust masks and goggles may also be useful. If you are indoors, close all windows and doors. Outdoors, check wind direction and head away from the smoke and ash.

Amazing Volcanoes

People have long been both frightened and fascinated by volcanoes. Volcanoes have enough force to create a huge mountain in just a few days. They can trigger other disasters, such as floods, earthquakes, avalanches, and tsunamis. On the other hand, volcanoes can create new land and fertile soil. People farm their sides, ski their slopes, or just admire these sites of terrible power. ★

A volcano called Mount Fuji is a well-known symbol of Japan. It is very popular with hikers and climbers.

True Statistics

Oldest volcano in the world: Probably Mount Etna, Italy (350,000 years)

Percentage of volcanic activity that is underwater: 75 percent

Largest volcano: Mauna Loa, Hawai`i – 13,680 ft. (4,170 m.) above sea level

People killed by volcanoes since 1700: More than 260,000

Highest recorded lava temperature: 2,200 °F (1,200 °C)

Most active volcano: Kilauea Volcano, Hawai`i or Stromboli, Italy

Most powerful recorded eruption: Tambora Volcano, Indonesia (April, 1815)

Did you find the truth?

(T) A volcano can affect the weather.

(F) Volcanic eruptions are always violent explosions.

Resources

Books

Buckwalter, Stephanie. *Volcanoes: Disaster and Survival* (Deadly Disasters). Berkeley Heights, NJ: Enslow, 2005.

Lindeen, Mary. *Anatomy of a Volcano* (Shockwave). New York: Children's Press, 2008.

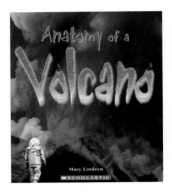

Rubin, Ken. *Volcanoes and Earthquakes*. New York: Simon & Schuster Children's Publishing, 2007.

Scholastic Books. *Our Changing Planet: How Volcanoes, Earthquakes, Tsunamis, and Weather Shape Our Planet* (Scholastic Voyages of Discovery). New York: Scholastic Inc., 1996.

Spilsbury, Louise and Richard. *Violent Volcanoes* (Awesome Forces of Nature). Chicago: Heinemann Library, 2004.

Trueit, Trudi Strain. *Volcanoes*. New York: Scholastic Inc., 2003.

van Rose, Susanna. *Volcano and Earthquake* (Eyewitness Books). New York: DK Children, 2008.

Organizations and Web Sites

National Geographic: Forces of Nature – Volcanoes
www.nationalgeographic.com/forcesofnature/interactive/
index.html?section=v
Explore all aspects of volcanoes. Make a volcano erupt online!

Learner: Can We Predict Volcanic Eruptions?
www.learner.org/interactives/volcanoes/entry.html
Learn about how scientists can forecast volcanoes, and view
online video clips from volcanic sites.

Geography for Kids: Volcanoes
www.geography4kids.com/files/earth_volcano.html
Read about different types of volcanoes and lava, then take
the quiz.

Places to Visit

Hawai`i Volcanoes National Park
P.O. Box 52
Hawai`i National Park,
HI 96718-0052
(808) 985 6000
www.nps.gov/havo/
Watch lava flow, and
complete an activities trail
to become a junior ranger.

Mount St. Helens Visitor Center at Silver Lake
3029 Spirit Lake Highway,
Castle Rock, WA 98611
(360) 274 0962
www.parks.wa.gov/
mountsthelens.asp
Explore interactive exhibits,
including a giant model of
Mount St. Helens.

Important Words

active volcano – a volcano that is erupting or has the potential to erupt

atmosphere (AT-muhss-fihr) – the layer of gases surrounding Earth or other planets

avalanche *(AV-uh-lanch)* – a large mass of snow or rock that suddenly falls down the side of a mountain

crust – the hard, outer layer of Earth or other solid planets

density – the weight of an object in relation to its size

evacuate (i-VAK-yoo-ate) – to leave a place because it may be too dangerous to stay there

geothermal (jee-oh-THUR-muhl) – having to do with the heat inside the earth

geyser (GYE-zur) – a jet of hot water and steam that bursts out regularly from a hot spring in a volcanic area

seismograph (SIZE-muh-graf) – an instrument that measures vibrations within Earth

tectonic plate – one of the large slabs of rock that make up Earth's outer crust

tiltmeter – an instrument used to measure tilting of Earth's surface; used by volcanologists on ground around a volcano

turbine – a wheel that is turned by moving water, steam, or gas

volcanologist – a scientist who studies volcanoes

Index

Page numbers in **bold** indicate illustrations

About the Author

Award-winning author Elaine Landau has a bachelor's degree from New York University and a master's degree in Library and Information Science. She has written more than 300 nonfiction books for children and young adults. Ms. Landau lives in Miami, Florida, with her husband and son. You can visit her at her Web site www.elainelandau.com.

PHOTOGRAPHS © 2008: Big Stock Photo (© Laurence Gough, p. 30; © Cheung Chi Man, p. 42); Corel (cover); Courtesy of Dipartimento di Ingegneria Elettrica Elettronica e dei Sistemi, Università degli Studi di Catania (p. 4; pp. 24–25); Getty Images (p. 20; pp. 40–41); iStockphoto.com (©Alena Yakusheva, p. 29); New Zealand Herald (p. 38); Photodisc (p.18); Photolibrary (p. 6; p. 8; p. 17; p. 26; p. 37); photonewzealand (Age Fotostock/Juan Carlos Munoz, p. 32; Alamy, p. 10); Tranz/Corbis (p. 9; p. 28; p. 31); U.S. Geological Survey (p. 15; D. Dzurisin, p. 34; Lyn Topinka, p. 21; T. J. Casadevall, Mt. Pinatubo, p. 23)

The publisher would like to thank Giovanni Muscato of the Dipartimento di Ingegneria Elettrica Elettronica e dei Sistemi, Università degli Studi di Catania, for the photo of the Robovolc on page 4, and pages 24–25.